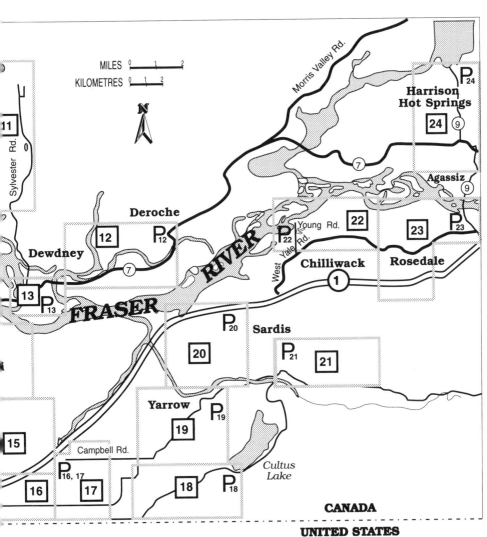

Bicycling Near Vancouver

BOOK ONE
The Central Fraser Valley

Margaret Slack

Gordon Soules Book Publishers Ltd.
West Vancouver, Canada
Seattle, U.S.

Canadian Cataloguing in Publication Data

Slack, Margaret, 1950-
Bicycling near Vancouver

Contents: Book 1, The Central Fraser Valley.
ISBN 0-919574-33-5 (v. 1)

1. Cycling—British Columbia—Vancouver Metropolitan Area-Guidebooks.
2. Vancouver Metropolitan Area (B.C.)—Guidebooks.   I. Title.
FC3847.18.S52 1994   796.6'4'0971133   C94-910756-5
F1089.5.V22S52 1994

Published in Canada by
Gordon Soules Book Publishers Ltd.
1352-B Marine Drive
West Vancouver, BC V7T 1B5

Published in the United States by
Gordon Soules Book Publishers Ltd.
620-1916 Pike Place
Seattle, WA 98101

Editing by Anne Norman
Designed by Harry Bardal
Typesetting by A.R. CompuType Graphics, Vancouver, BC, Canada
Printed and bound in Canada by Hignell Printing Limited

Contents

Acknowledgments

My sincere thanks and appreciation to my parents, Hermine and Peter Driessen, for setting aside many hours to help with the research for each route.

Others who encouraged me and contributed valuable ideas were my sons, Craig and Kevin; my brother, Peter Driessen; Gordon Soules; Elsa Drinkle; Wolfgang Wenzel; and Claire Alston.

Legend for the 24 Route Maps

≡ Primary highway
(high volume—
bicycling prohibited)

═ Secondary highway
(medium-high volume)

▄▄ Paved bike route

■■ Unpaved bike route

├─┤ Railway

◄◄◄ Difficult grade
(arrows point uphill)

◄◄◄ Route direction

■ ■ ■ Unpaved road/dike

 Walking trails

? Information

 Lodging

G Groceries

 Food services

👥 Washroom

🚲 Bike store

🎋 Picnic

🏊 Swimming

◆ Point of interest

P Parking

- - · - Canada/US border

5

Route 1: Pitt Polder

Flat, open, paved roads with approximately 11 km of rough, unpaved dikes crisscrossing marshy terrain of a bird sanctuary . . . red-tail hawks, eagles, sandhill cranes, great blue herons . . . wide-open countryside . . . distant peaks of the Coast Mountain Range . . . green pastures . . . songbirds . . . blueberry fields . . . nurseries . . . canoe rentals, (604) 465-7820

Round trip   33 km (20.5 miles)

Traffic   Low volume

Parking   Harris Road, just south of the Alouette River; large gravel area on the east side of the road

Annual events

In Maple Ridge
May: Mountain Festival, Maple Ridge, (604) 467-7255
July: Canada Day, Maple Ridge Parks, (604) 463-5221

In Pitt Meadows
June: Pitt Meadows Days, (604) 465-7820
July: Canada Day, Pitt Meadows Parks, (604) 465-5454
August: Pitt Meadows Blueberry Festival, (604) 465-5454

For further information on events and attractions in the Maple Ridge area and Pitt Meadows area, contact the Maple Ridge Travel Infocentre at (604) 463-3366 or the Pitt Meadows Travel Infocentre at (604) 465-7820.

Did you know?
In 1951, Dutch immigrant engineers improved the efficiency of the dike system along the Alouette River and Pitt River so that the land could then be farmed. Polder is a word of Dutch origin and refers to low-lying land reclaimed from a body of water.

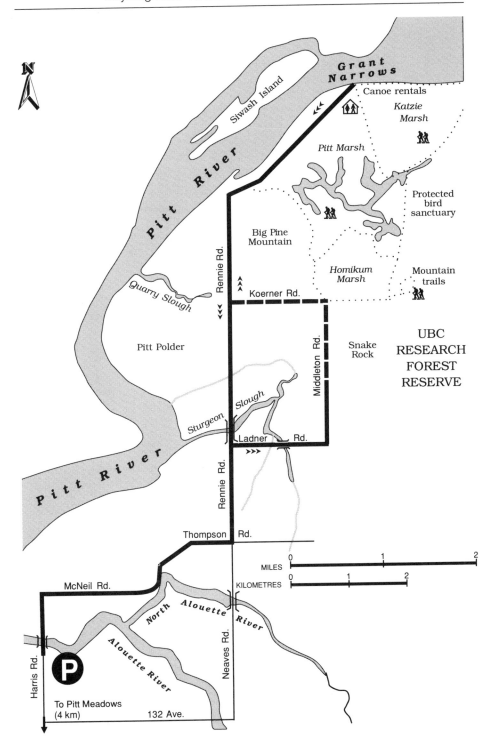

Route 2: Kanaka Creek

A variety of ups and downs on paved roads . . . a challenging ride along forested, winding paved roads . . . country lanes . . . beautifully landscaped country estates . . . distant views of the peaks of Golden Ears Mountain . . . river and valley views . . . Bell-Irving Fish Hatchery (11450—256th Street)

Round trip 36 km (22 miles)

Traffic Low to medium volume

Parking Maple Ridge Park, on 232nd Street

Annual events

In Whonnock
September: Whonnock Days, Whonnock Community Centre, (604) 462-8212
In Ruskin
September: Ruskin Old Fashioned Fall Fair, Ruskin Community Hall, 96th Avenue at 284th Street, (604) 462-9091 / 462-7596

For more information on events and attractions in the area, contact the Maple Ridge Travel Infocentre at (604) 463-3366.

Did you know?
The native people who lived along the riverbank where Whonnock now stands gave the village its name, which means "the place of the humpback salmon." When the first non-native settlers, mostly British and Norwegian, arrived in the 1880s, the only way to reach Whonnock was by steamboat; later the railway became a vital link.

Connecting routes
Route 3: Whonnock Lake
Route 4: Fort Langley–Derby Reach (take the Albion ferry)
Route 5: Fort Langley–Telegraph Trail (take the Albion ferry)

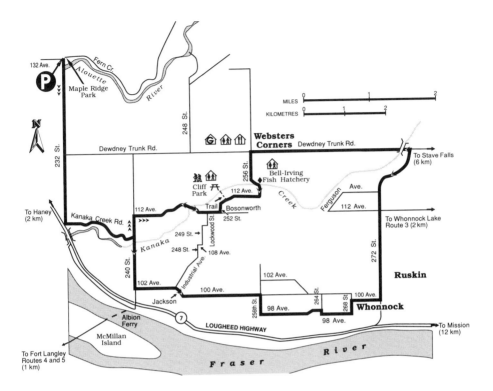

Route 3: Whonnock Lake

Some very steep hills and narrow paved roads . . . rural, forested, shady, winding roads . . . Railway Trail, a lakeside unpaved trail connecting two B.C. Hydro dam sites . . . swimming in Whonnock Lake

Round trip   15 km (9 miles) loop or 25 km (15.5 miles) including Railway Trail

Traffic   Low to medium volume

Parking   Whonnock Lake Park, off 276th Street

Annual events

In Whonnock
September: Whonnock Days, Whonnock Community Centre (604) 462-8212
In Ruskin
September: Ruskin Old Fashioned Fall Fair, Ruskin Community Hall, 96th Avenue at 284th Street, (604) 462-9091 / 462-7596

For further information on events and attractions in the area, contact the Maple Ridge Travel Infocentre at (604) 463-3366.

Connecting route
Route 2: Kanaka Creek

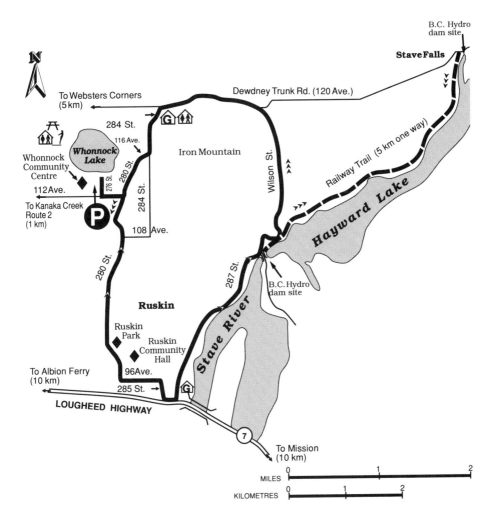

Route 4: Fort Langley–Derby Reach

Mostly easy ups and downs on paved roads . . . historic village of Fort Langley with restaurants, antiques, crafts, clothing shops . . . Fort Langley National Historic Park, recreating with replica structures the original Hudson's Bay Company trading post, (604) 888-4424 . . . glimpses of Canada's pioneering past at the Langley Centennial Museum, (604) 888-3922, and B.C. Farm Machinery Museum, (604) 888-2273 . . . the original site of the Hudson's Bay Company fort on Allard Crescent, now marked by a plaque . . . the restored, circa 1909 home (not open to the public) of Alex Houston, one of the first European settlers in the area . . . wooded trails in Derby Reach Regional Park, (604) 888-1477 . . . diked cranberry bogs

Round trip   20 km (12 miles)

Traffic   Light to moderate, with possibility of heavier traffic on 88th Avenue and 96th Avenue during certain times of the day

Parking   Marina Park in Fort Langley (see inset on map)

Annual events

In Fort Langley
May: May Day Celebrations, village of Fort Langley
July: Canada Day Celebrations, village of Fort Langley
August: Fort Festival of the Performing Arts, Fort Langley Community Hall
August: Brigade Days, Fort Langley National Historic Park
August: Artists at Work, village of Fort Langley
September: Harvest Festival, Langley Centennial Museum, (604) 888-3922

For further information on events and attractions in the area, contact the Fort Langley Travel Infocentre at (604) 888-1477.

Connecting routes
Route 2: Kanaka Creek (take the Albion ferry)
Route 5: Fort Langley–Telegraph Trail
Route 6: Glen Valley

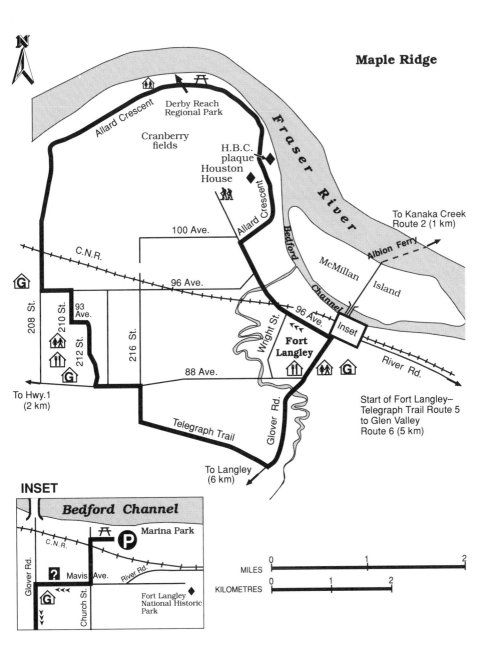

Maple Ridge

Derby Reach
Regional Park

Allard Crescent

Cranberry
fields

H.B.C.
plaque
Houston
House

Fraser River

To Kanaka Creek
Route 2 (1 km)

100 Ave.

Allard Crescent

C.N.R.

96 Ave.

Bedford Channel

McMillan

Albion Ferry

Island

208 St.

210 St.

93
Ave.

212 St.

216 St.

Wright St.

96 Ave.

Inset

Fort
Langley

88 Ave.

River Rd.

To Hwy.1
(2 km)

Glover Rd.

Telegraph Trail

Start of Fort Langley–
Telegraph Trail Route 5
to Glen Valley
Route 6 (5 km)

To Langley
(6 km)

INSET

Bedford Channel

C.N.R.

Marina Park

Glover Rd.

Mavis Ave.

River Rd.

Church St.

Fort Langley
National Historic
Park

MILES 0   1   2

KILOMETRES 0   1   2

Route 5: Fort Langley–Telegraph Trail

Mostly easy ups and downs on paved roads, except for a relatively steep climb to Telegraph Trail . . . mountain and river views

Round trip   20 km (12 miles)

Traffic   Low to medium volume

Parking   Marina Park in Fort Langley (see inset on map)

Annual events

In Fort Langley
May: May Day Celebrations, village of Fort Langley
July: Canada Day Celebrations, village of Fort Langley
August: Fort Festival of the Performing Arts, Fort Langley Community Hall
August: Brigade Days, Fort Langley National Historic Park
August: Artists at Work, village of Fort Langley
September: Harvest Festival, Langley Centennial Museum, (604) 888-3922

For further information on events and attractions in the area, contact the Fort Langley Travel Infocentre at (604) 888-1477.

Did you know?
Telegraph Trail is part of the attempted overland route of the transcontinental telegraph, started in 1865. The route was to connect Moscow to New York via Siberia, the Bering Strait, the Northwest Coast, and continental United States. In 1866, communications cable was laid under the Atlantic Ocean, making the telegraph project obsolete.

Connecting routes
Route 2: Kanaka Creek (take the Albion ferry)
Route 4: Fort Langley–Derby Reach
Route 6: Glen Valley

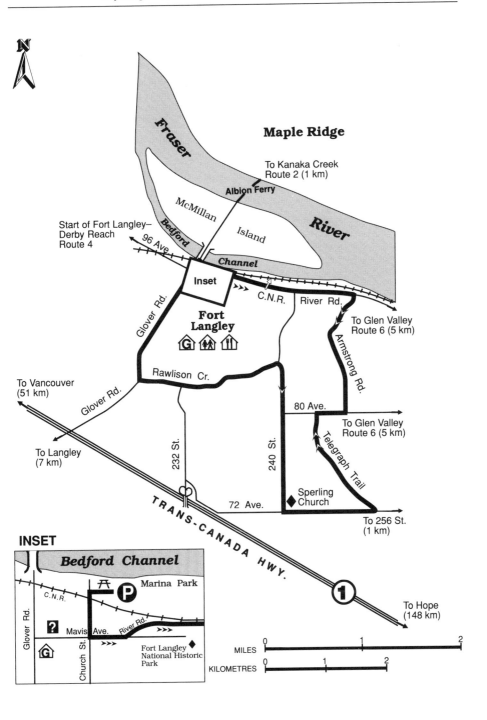

N

Maple Ridge

To Kanaka Creek
Route 2 (1 km)

Albion Ferry

McMillan

Island

River

Fraser

Bedford

Start of Fort Langley–
Derby Reach
Route 4

96 Ave.

Channel

Inset

C.N.R.   River Rd.

Glover Rd.

Fort
Langley

To Glen Valley
Route 6 (5 km)

Armstrong Rd.

Rawlison Cr.

To Vancouver
(51 km)

Glover Rd.

80 Ave.

To Glen Valley
Route 6 (5 km)

To Langley
(7 km)

232 St.

240 St.

Telegraph Trail

Sperling
Church

72 Ave.

To 256 St.
(1 km)

INSET

Bedford Channel

C.N.R.

Marina Park

P

Glover Rd.

Mavis Ave.

River Rd.

Church St.

Fort Langley
National Historic
Park

MILES

KILOMETRES

TRANS-CANADA HWY.

1

To Hope
(148 km)

0   1   2

0   1   2

15

Route 6: Glen Valley

A variety of ups and downs on paved roads, with some very steep grades, including a thrilling ride down Lefeuvre Road toward the banks of the Fraser River . . . quiet country lanes . . . distant mountain views . . . wild blackberries

Round trip   26 km (16 miles)

Traffic   Low volume on most of the route

Parking   On wide paved shoulder of the west side of 264th Street, north of Highway 1, close to the overpass

Annual events

In nearby Fort Langley
May: May Day Celebrations, village of Fort Langley
July: Canada Day Celebrations, village of Fort Langley
August: Fort Festival of the Performing Arts, Fort Langley Community Hall
August: Brigade Days, Fort Langley National Historic Park
August: Artists at Work, village of Fort Langley
September: Harvest Festival, Langley Centennial Museum,(604) 888-3922

For further information on events and attractions in the area, contact the Fort Langley Travel Infocentre at (604) 888-1477.

Did you know?
The Langley Naturalists' Society wants to conserve the remaining agricultural land in the Glen Valley. A planned trail system for horses, cyclists, and walkers would run through Glen Valley to Sumas Mountain. For more information, call the Corporation of the Township of Langley, Parks and Recreation Department, at (604) 530-1323.

Connecting routes
Route 4: Fort Langley–Derby Reach
Route 5: Fort Langley–Telegraph Trail
Route 7: Bradner
Route 8: Aldergrove

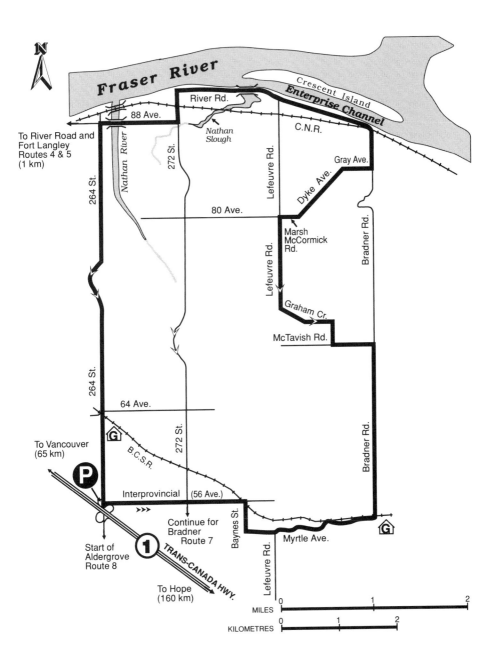

Route 7: Bradner

Paved roads with some steep grades . . . views of the mountain peaks to the north and Mount Baker to the south . . . historic Bradner store, built in 1911 . . . fields of tulips and daffodils . . . fresh vegetables, strawberries, raspberries, blueberries, and cut flowers at roadside stands . . . Christmas tree farms . . . deer sometimes seen in wooded areas . . . beautifully landscaped country estates

Round trip   24.5 km (15 miles)

Traffic   Low volume on most of the route

Parking   On wide paved shoulder of the west side of 264th Street, north of Highway 1, close to the overpass

Annual events

In Bradner
April: Bradner Flower Show, Bradner Community Centre

For further information on events and attractions in the area, contact the Langley Travel Infocentre at (604) 530-6656.

Did you know?

In the early 1900s, several lumber mills provided employment for the settlers, one of whom was George Pratt, who built the Bradner store.

Connecting routes

Route 6: Glen Valley
Route 8: Aldergrove

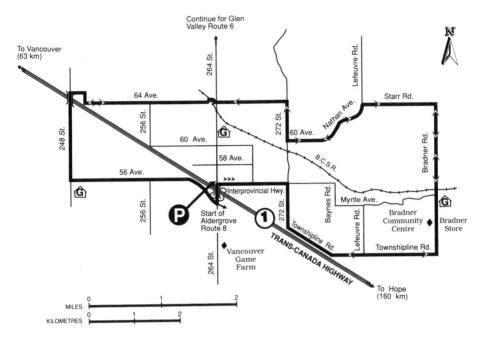

Route 8: Aldergrove

Paved roads with some steep sections . . . mostly through farmland . . . views of Mount Baker to the south and Golden Ears Mountain to the north . . . farmers' fruit stalls selling strawberries and raspberries . . . Aldergrove Lake Regional Park, (604) 856-8383, accessed via 8th Avenue, with playing fields, picnic facilities, an artificial lake for swimming, and hiking trails through forests . . . nearby on 264th Street (Highway 13), Vancouver Game Farm, (604) 856-6825, with over one hundred species of animals from every continent

Round trip 22 km (13.5 miles)

Traffic Low to medium volume; Monday to Friday, watch for gravel trucks along 8th Avenue between Lefeuvre Road and 272nd Street

Parking On wide paved shoulder of the west side of 264th Street, north of Highway 1, close to the overpass

Annual events

In Aldergrove
June: Aldergrove Festival Days, (604) 856-8383
September: Aldergrove Fall Fair, (604) 856-8383

For further information on events and attractions in the area, call the Fort Langley Travel Infocentre at (604) 888-1477.

Did you know?

Aldergrove Festival Days began in 1912 and is one of the oldest agricultural fairs in British Columbia.

Connecting routes

Route 6: Glen Valley
Route 7: Bradner
Route 9: South Langley
Route 10: Campbell Valley

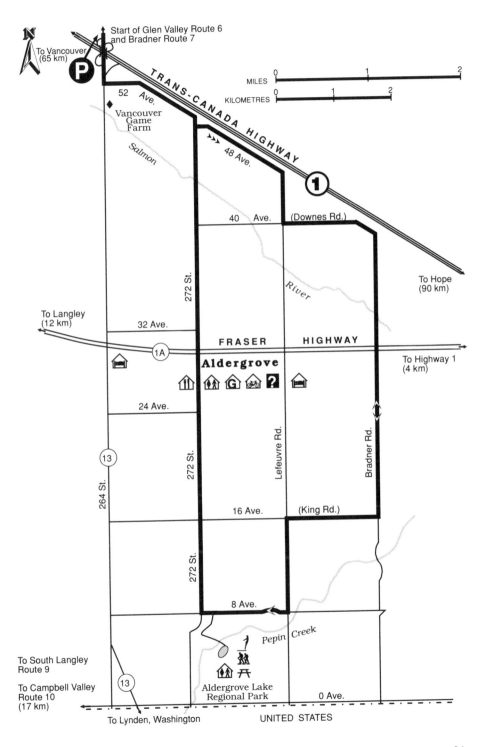

Route 9: South Langley

Paved roads with some steep grades . . . colorful nurseries . . . lakeside estates . . . farms with thoroughbreds . . . Campbell Valley Regional Park, home to wildlife (including shrews and owls) and with hiking trails, horseback riding, and picnic facilities

Round trip   44 km (27 miles)

Traffic   Low to medium volume

Parking   Campbell Valley Regional Park, South Valley entrance at 204th Street and 8th Avenue

Annual events

In Campbell Valley Regional Park
July/August: Summer Fun in the Sun, (604) 530-4983
September: Celebration of Nature, (604) 530-4983
September: 49th to Fraser Relay, (604) 530-1323

For further information on events and attractions in the area, contact the Langley Travel Infocentre at (604) 530-6656.

Did you know?

In 1875, a pioneer named Vanetta constructed the Old Yale Road for transporting produce from the Fraser Valley to New Westminster and Vancouver. From the end of this road at the Fraser River, a ferry service floated wagon teams across to New Westminster.

Connecting routes

Route 8: Aldergrove
Route 10: Campbell Valley

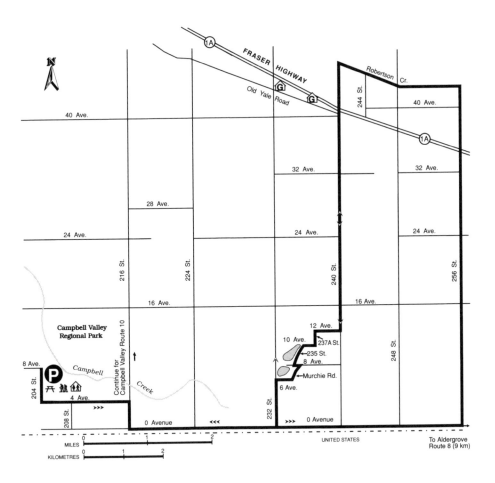

Route 10: Campbell Valley

Quiet, paved country roads . . . at 710—204th Street, the old Lochiel Schoolhouse (built in 1924) and the restored Annand/Rowlatt Heritage Farmhouse (built in 1886 and currently maintained by a live-in caretaker) . . . glimpses of lakeside estates . . . in Campbell Valley Regional Park, winding woodland walking trails and marsh boardwalks (no bicycles allowed)

Round trip 24 km (15 miles)

Traffic Low volume except for high volume on 16th Avenue

Parking Campbell Valley Regional Park, South Valley entrance at 204th Street and 8th Avenue

Annual events

In Campbell Valley Regional Park
July and August: Summer Fun in the Sun, (604) 530-4983
September: Celebration of Nature, (604) 530-4983
September: 49th to Fraser Relay, (604) 530-1323

For further information on events and attractions in the area, contact the Langley Travel Infocentre at (604) 530-6656.

Connecting routes
Route 8: Aldergrove
Route 9: South Langley

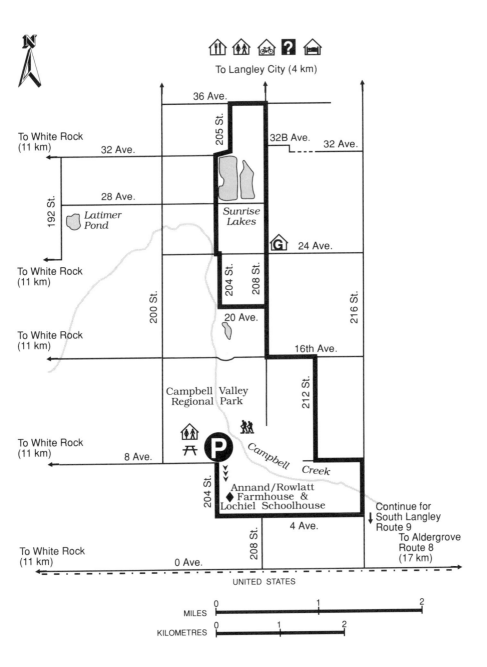

Route 11: Hatzic Prairie

Varies between flat paved stretches south of Durieu Road and steep paved sections north of Durieu Road . . . quiet rural countryside . . . valley views . . . nearby mountain peaks . . . a variety of small farms

Round trip   16 km (10 miles)

Traffic   Low to medium volume

Parking   Hatzic Prairie Community Hall, on Farms Road

Annual events

In nearby Mission
May to October: Dragstrip races, Mission Raceways, (604) 826-6315
June to August: Twilight concerts, Fraser River Heritage Park, 2 km east of downtown Mission, north of the Lougheed Highway, (604) 826-0277
July: Canada Day Celebrations
July: International Pow Wow, St. Mary's Centre, 2 km east of downtown Mission, on the Lougheed Highway, (604) 826-1281
July: Mission Folk Music Festival, Fraser River Heritage Park, 2 km east of downtown Mission, north of the Lougheed Highway, (604) 826-0277
July: Agricultural Fair, Mission Leisure Centre, (604) 826-6914

For further information on events and attractions in the area, contact the Mission Regional Travel Infocentre at (604) 826-6914.

Did you know?

Mission got its name in 1861 when Father Fouquet, an Oblate priest, came from France to start a school and a mission. This school was situated where the Fraser Valley Heritage Park in Mission is today.

Connecting routes

Route 12: Nicomen Island (follow Sylvester Road south to the Lougheed Highway)
Route 13: Dewdney (follow Sylvester Road south to the Lougheed Highway)

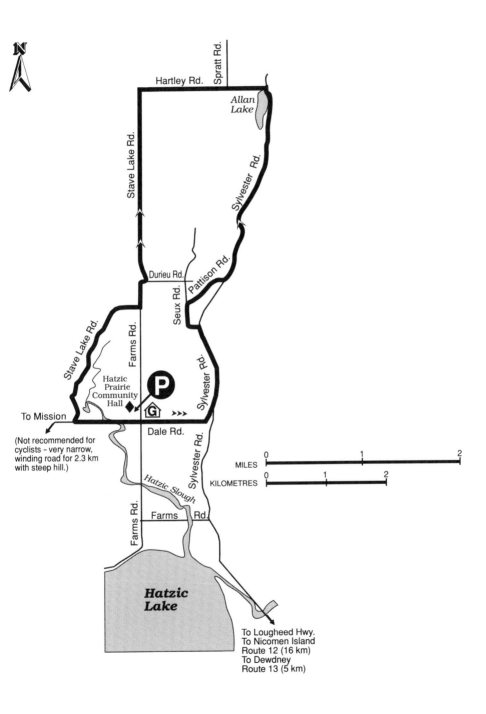

Route 12: Nicomen Island

Flat paved roads with approximately 5 km of unpaved dikes . . . peaceful surroundings . . . wide open spaces . . . undeveloped waterfront of the Nicomen Slough and the Fraser River . . . fields of Queen Anne's lace in July . . . eagles migrating to the area to feast on salmon and small rodents from December to February . . . trumpeter swans and great blue herons gathering along the shores of the slow-moving Nicomen Slough

Round trip   25 km (15.5 miles)

Traffic   Low volume

Parking   In Deroche, on north side of Nicomen Slough; gravel area beside the railway tracks on North Nicomen Road

Annual events

In nearby Mission
May to October: Dragstrip races, Mission Raceways, (604) 826-6315
June to August: Twilight concerts, Fraser River Heritage Park, 2 km east of downtown Mission, north of the Lougheed Highway, (604) 826-0277
July: Canada Day Celebrations July: International Pow Wow, St. Mary's Centre, 2 km east of downtown Mission, on the Lougheed Highway, (604) 826-1281
July: Mission Folk Music Festival, Fraser River Heritage Park, 2 km east of downtown Mission, north of the Lougheed Highway, (604) 826-0277
July: Agricultural Fair, Mission Leisure Centre, (604) 826-6914

In Deroche
July: Deroche Days, (604) 826-6914

For further information on events and attractions in the area, contact the Mission Regional Travel Infocentre at (604) 826-6914.

Did you know?
The name of Nicomen Island is derived from the native word *Nikoamin,* for which there are two possible meanings: ''water going around'' or ''near a big creek.'' Europeans settled in Nicomen in the 1860s, and the area was subject to much flooding later in the century.

Connecting routes
Route 11: Hatzic Prairie
Route 13: Dewdney

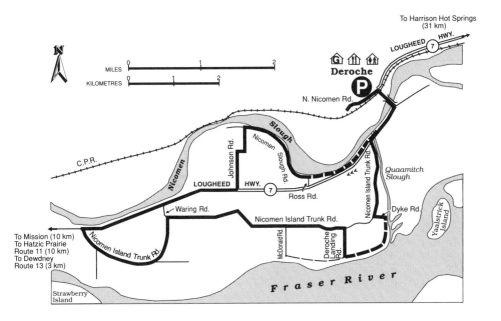

Route 13: Dewdney

Flat, quiet, paved country roads with 3 km of unpaved dikes . . . scenic Fraser River views . . . birdwatching . . . Dewdney Nature Regional Park on the Fraser River (no swimming) . . . nearby, east of Mission, Fraser River Heritage Park, (604) 826-0277, with historic ruins of St. Mary's Mission and Indian Residential School (To reach the park, travel west on the Lougheed Highway, turn north onto Stave Lake Road, and then turn east onto Fifth Avenue, which leads into the parking lot of the park.)

Round trip   9 km (5.5 miles)

Traffic   Low volume

Parking   Dewdney Nature Regional Park, on River Road South

Annual events

In nearby Mission
May to October: Dragstrip Races, Mission Raceways, (604) 826-6315
June to August: Twilight concerts, Fraser River Heritage Park, 2 km east of downtown Mission, north of the Lougheed Highway, (604) 826-0277
July: Canada Day Celebrations
July: International Pow Wow, St. Mary's Centre, 2 km east of downtown Mission, on the Lougheed Highway, (604) 826-1281
July: Mission Folk Music Festival, Fraser River Heritage Park, 2 km east of downtown Mission, north of the Lougheed Highway, (604) 826-0277
July: Agricultural Fair, Mission Leisure Centre, (604) 826-6914

For further information on events and attractions in the area, contact the Mission Regional Travel Infocentre at (604) 826-6914.

Connecting routes
Route 11: Hatzic Prairie
Route 12: Nicomen Island

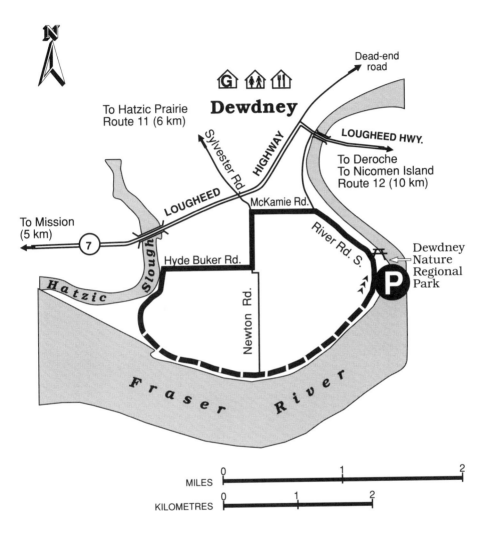

Route 14: Matsqui Trail Regional Park

Mostly flat, quiet, paved country roads with 6 km of picturesque, unpaved dike trail . . . sightings of parachute jumpers . . . views of the distinctive bell tower of Westminster Abbey in Mission . . . Fraser River views . . . wild blackberries . . . blueberry farms, such as Makara Blueberry Farms, 5331 Riverside Road, (604) 859-4797 / 859-1735

Round trip   15 km (9 miles)

Traffic   Low volume

Parking   Matsqui Trail Regional Park on the south side of the Mission bridge

Annual events

In nearby Abbotsford
July: Abbotsford Berry Festival
August: The Flight Begins Airshow Week
August: Abbotsford International Airshow, Abbotsford Airport, Airshow Society, (604) 852-8511
August: Matsqui Centennial Heritage Festival, Trethewey House heritage site, Abbotsford

For further information about events and attractions in the area, contact the Abbotsford-Matsqui Travel Infocentre at (604) 859-9651.

Connecting route
Route 15: Clayburn

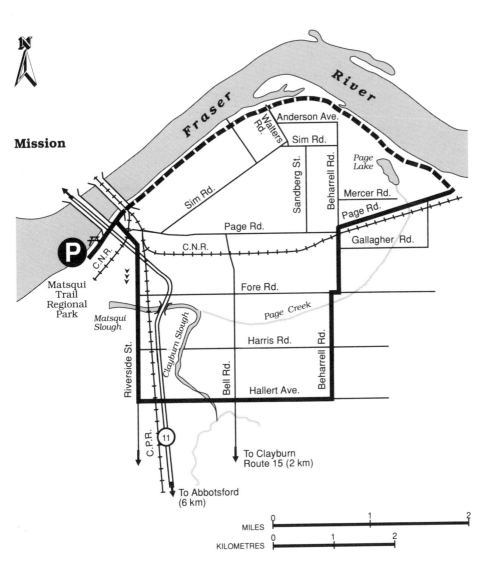

Route 15: Clayburn

Some steep hills on paved roads with 2 km of unpaved roads . . . small hillside farms . . . cultivated blueberry farms . . . wild blackberry bushes . . . forested, shady, steep, winding paved roads . . . very hilly countryside . . . glimpses of snowcapped Mount Baker . . . mixture of residential areas and quiet country roads

Round trip 22 km (14 miles)

Traffic Low volume on most of the route

Parking Clayburn Road opposite the Old Clayburn Village Store

Annual events

In Clayburn
July: Heritage Day, Old Clayburn Village Store, (604) 853-4020

For further information on events and attractions in the area, contact the Abbotsford Travel Infocentre at (604) 859-9651.

Did you know?
Clayburn, founded in 1905, was the first company town in British Columbia. The Vancouver Fire and Clay Company built a row of houses around a brickyard of sheds and kilns. Bricks that built the Vancouver Hotel and the old CPR station (now the Seabus terminal) were fired here. The plant was shut down in the 1930s. Fewer than two hundred people live here now.

Connecting route
Route 14: Matsqui Trail Regional Park

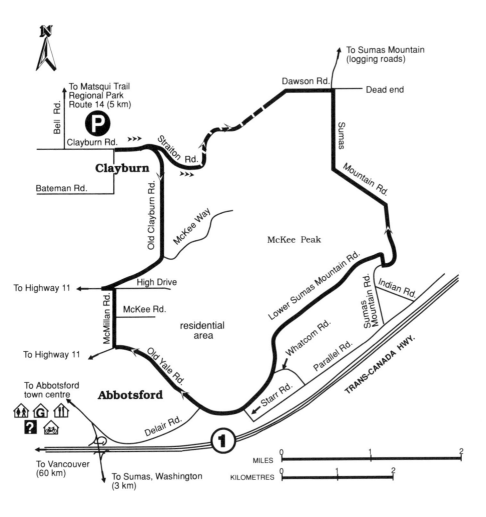

Route 16: Sumas Prairie–Sumas Slough

Similar to Route 17, Sumas Prairie–Old Yale Road, with winding, scenic, flat, paved country roads . . . wide-open spaces . . . glimpses of Mount Baker to the south and Mount Vedder to the east . . . immaculately maintained farms . . . silos . . . serene Hougen Park alongside the Sumas Slough

Round trip 19 km (12 miles)

Traffic Low volume

Parking Cole Road rest area at exit #99 going east on Trans-Canada Highway 1

Annual events

In Hougen Park
July: Sumas Day, Hougen Park

For further information on events and attractions in the area, contact the Abbotsford Travel Infocentre at (604) 859-9651.

Connecting routes
Route 17: Sumas Prairie–Old Yale Road
Route 19: Yarrow

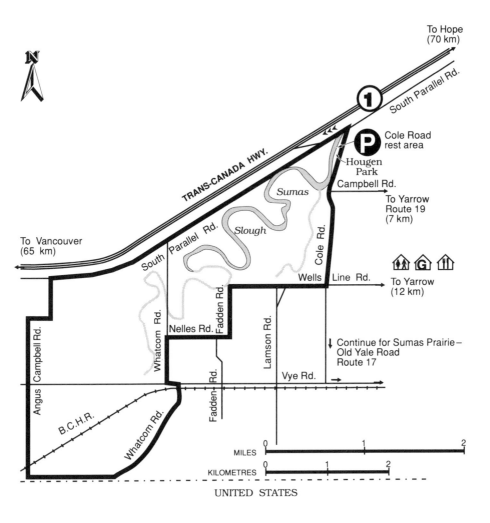

Route 17: Sumas Prairie–Old Yale Road

Similar to Route 16, Sumas Prairie–Sumas Slough, with winding, scenic, flat, paved country roads . . . wide-open spaces . . . glimpses of Mount Baker to the south and Mount Vedder to the east . . . immaculately maintained farms . . . silos . . . serene Hougen Park alongside the Sumas Slough

Round trip   20 km (12.5 miles)

Traffic   Low volume

Parking   Cole Road rest area at exit #99 going east on Trans-Canada Highway 1

Annual events

In Hougen Park
July: Sumas Day, Hougen Park

For further information on events and attractions in the area, contact the Abbotsford Travel Infocentre at (604) 859-9651.

Connecting routes
Route 16: Sumas Prairie–Sumas Slough
Route 19: Yarrow

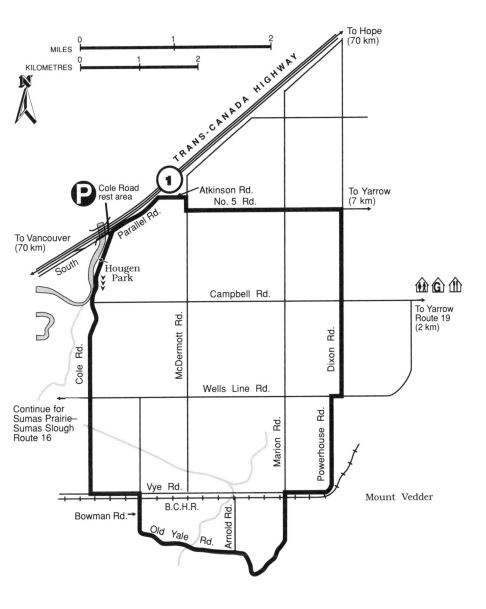

Route 18: Columbia Valley–Cultus Lake

Easy rolling hills on paved roads, with 1.5 km of steep unpaved roads . . . beaches of popular Cultus Lake . . . spring lambs and beehives in picturesque farm fields . . . . raspberry fields . . . cottonwood trees . . . views to the United States, including a highly visible mountainside cut of trees that indicates the border between Canada and the United States

Round trip   24 km (15 miles)

Traffic   Low volume on most of the route

Parking   Parking lot at Maple Bay picnic area

Annual events

In the Cultus Lake area
June: Indian Festival, Cultus Lake Main Beach
July: Krafty Raft Race, Cultus Lake Main Beach
August: Columbia Valley Logger Sports, Columbia Valley Community Centre, 1202 Kossikar Road
August: Beach Party, Cultus Lake Main Beach

For further information on events and attractions in the area, contact the Chilliwack Travel Infocentre at (604) 858-8121 or toll-free at 1-800-665-6556.

Did you know?

Native people believed that a dreaded supernatural creature lived in Cultus Lake. *Cultus* is Chinook jargon for "worthless."

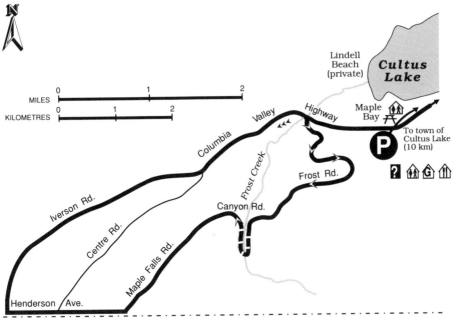

Route 19: Yarrow

Winding, uphill paved road to start, then mostly flat paved roads, and approximately 4 km of rough, unpaved dikes . . . Sumas Prairie views . . . dairy farms . . . goose farm . . . guided farm tours at The Apple Farm, where twenty-two varieties of apples and nine varieties of pears are grown on dwarf trees, never growing much higher than two metres, 4490 Boundary Road, (604) 823-4311

Round trip   19 km (12 miles)

Traffic   Low to medium volume

Parking   Majuba Heritage Park, on Majuba Hill Road (Old Yale Road)

Annual events

In Yarrow
June: Yarrow Days, (604) 823-6324

For further information on events and attractions in the area, contact the Chilliwack Travel Infocentre at (604) 858-8121 or toll-free at 1-800-665-6556.

Connecting routes
Route 16: Sumas Prairie–Sumas Slough
Route 17: Sumas Prairie–Old Yale Road
Route 20: Vedder Canal

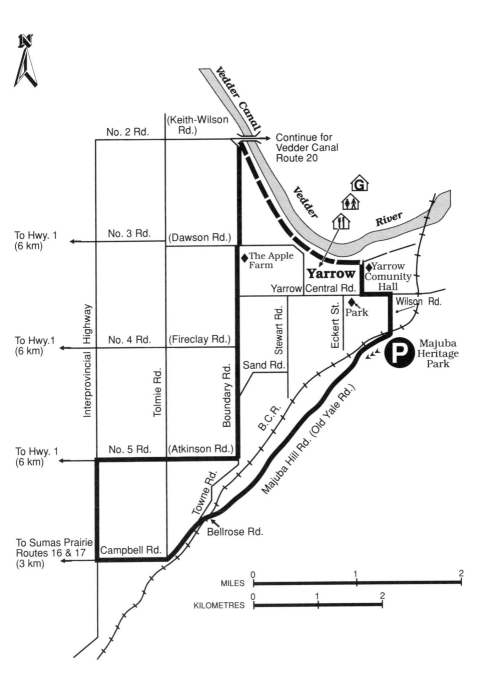

Route 20: Vedder Canal

Mostly flat, quiet, paved country roads with approximately 5 km of unpaved dikes
. . . gently flowing Vedder Canal . . . views of Sumas Mountain to the northwest, Mount Cheam to the east . . . chestnut trees . . . willow trees . . . the occasional hang glider

Round trip   21 km (13 miles)

Traffic   Low volume, except for Lickman Road and Keith-Wilson Road, where the volume is moderate

Parking   Chilliwack Travel Infocentre on Luckakuck Way; unpaved parking area

Annual events

In Chilliwack area
August: Atchelitz Threshermen's Association Steam Expo, corner of Lickman Road and Trans-Canada Highway 1, (604) 823-2119 / 823-6303
September: Chilliwack Bluegrass Festival
September: Atchelitz Threshermen's Association Antique Powerland, corner of Lickman Road and Trans-Canada Highway 1, (604) 792-2069

For further information on events and attractions in the area, contact the Chilliwack Travel Infocentre at (604) 858-8121 or toll-free at 1-800-665-6556.

Did you know?
Before 1919, the land between Vedder Canal and Abbotsford was lake and marsh. The Vedder Canal, completed in 1924, made 11,700 ha (29,000 acres) of prime farmland available for cultivation.

Connecting route
Route 19: Yarrow

Route 21: Sardis–Elkview Road

A challenging route with steep, winding paved roads and 8 km of unpaved roads and variable grades, from gently rolling to steep . . . mountain meadows . . . old abandoned orchards . . . waterfalls . . . fields of hops

Round trip   25 km (15.5 miles)

Traffic   Low volume once outside the town of Sardis

Parking   Sardis Park, on Manuel Road

Annual events

In Chilliwack
April: Pacific Northwest Square Dance Festival, at various locations
August: International Dew Worm Races (fun for the family) at Ryder Lake Farmers' and Women's Institute Hall, Elkview Road, (604) 858-4511

For further information on events and attractions in the area, contact the Chilliwack Travel Infocentre at (604) 858-8121 or toll-free at 1-800-665-6556.

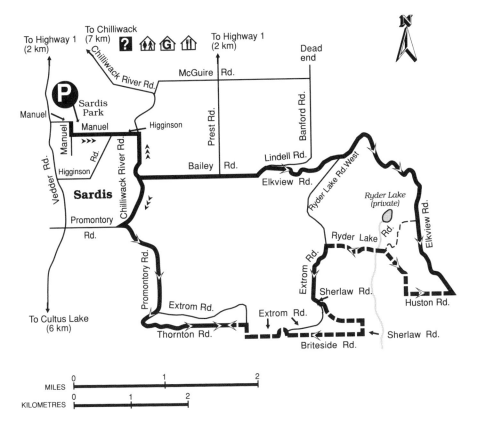

Route 22: Chilliwack–Banks of the Fraser River

Flat, winding paved roads along the Fraser River . . . rich agricultural fields . . . large and small dairy farms . . . Christmas tree farms . . . fields of hops . . . magnificent old maple and willow trees lining the roads

Round trip   33 km (20.5 miles)

Traffic   Low volume on most of the route

Parking   Island 22 Campground and picnic area at the end of Cartmell Road, a 1.5 km (1 mile) gravel road, off Young Road North

Annual events

In Chilliwack and area
May: Country Living Days Parade, downtown Chilliwack, (604) 858-8121
July: Chilliwack Country Music Festival, Island 22 Campground, (604) 792-7155

For further information on events and attractions in the area, contact the Chilliwack Travel Infocentre at (604) 858-8121 or toll-free at 1-800-665-6556.

Did you know?
Minto Landing, no longer accessible, came into significance when Jeff Harrison and Bob Menton established a mail and passenger ferry service between Harrison Mills and Chilliwack soon after the completion of the CPR in 1886.

Connecting route
Route 23: Rosedale

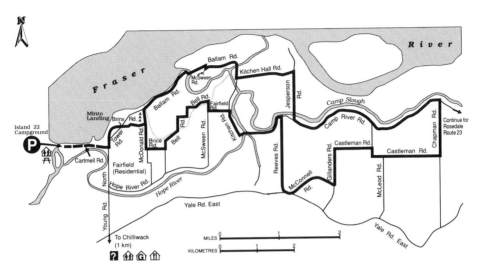

Route 23: Rosedale

Flat, scenic, winding paved roads . . . small tree farms . . . dairy farms . . . hazelnut farms . . . driveways lined with poplars . . . turf farms . . . farm tours at nearby Double D Acres, 52300 Allan Road, Rosedale, (604) 794-7335 . . . fields of hops, corn, and sunflowers in August . . . view of Bridal Veil Falls to the south . . . wooded areas along the fast-flowing Fraser River

Round trip 27 km (17 miles)

Traffic Low to medium volume

Parking Rosedale Community Park (within Ferry Island Provincial Park) on Ferry Island Road (see inset on map)

Annual events

In Rosedale
May: Rosedale Canoe Races, (604) 858-8121

For further information on events and attractions in the area, contact the Chilliwack Travel Infocentre at (604) 858-8121 or toll-free at 1-800-665-6556.

Did you know?
Rosedale was named after the wild roses that grow in abundance nearby.

Connecting route
Route 22: Chilliwack–Banks of the Fraser River

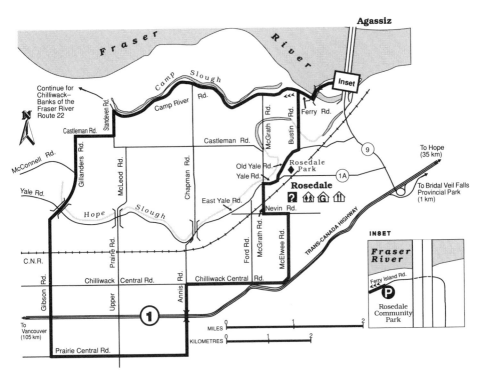

Agassiz

F r a s e r   R i v e r

Camp   *Slough*

Inset

Continue for
Chilliwack–
Banks of the
Fraser River
Route 22

Camp River Rd.

Standeven Rd.

Ferry Rd.

Castleman Rd.

Castleman Rd.

McGrath Rd.

Bustin Rd.

McConnell Rd.

Gillanders Rd.

Old Yale Rd.

Rosedale
Park

9

To Hope
(35 km)

Yale Rd.

McLeod Rd.

Chapman Rd.

Yale Rd.

1A

Rosedale

To Bridal Veil Falls
Provincial Park
(1 km)

Hope   *Slough*

East Yale Rd.

Nevin Rd.

INSET

*Fraser
River*

C.N.R.

Prairie Rd.

Ford Rd.

McGrath Rd.

McElwee Rd.

TRANS-CANADA HIGHWAY

Ferry Island Rd.

Gibson Rd.

Chilliwack Central Rd.

Annis Rd.

Chilliwack Central Rd.

Rosedale
Community
Park

1

To
Vancouver
(105 km)

MILES

KILOMETRES

Prairie Central Rd.

Route 24: Harrison Hot Springs

Quiet, mostly flat, paved country roads with some rolling hills . . . popular Harrison Lake . . . world famous hot springs . . . sandy beaches . . . swimming . . . soaking in the indoor hot springs public pool, (604) 796-2244 . . . lush pastoral countryside . . . rolling green pastures . . . farm tours by appointment at nearby Barcelona Hazelnut Farms in Agassiz, (604) 796-2555 . . . Agassiz-Harrison Museum, (604) 796-3545

Round trip   22 km (13.5 miles)

Traffic   Low to medium volume

Parking   In the village of Harrison Hot Springs on Lillooet Road in designated parking areas

Annual events

In Harrison Hot Springs
May: Can/Am Power Boat racing, Harrison Lake, (604) 796-3425
June: Kite Festival, Harrison Beach, (604) 796-3421
June: Paddlers' Rendezvous, Harrison Beach
July: Harrison Festival of the Arts, Harrison, (604) 796-3664
August: Kids' Sand Castle competition, Harrison Beach, (604) 796-2084
September: World Championship Sand Sculpture, Harrison Beach, (604) 796-3425
September: Agassiz Fall Fair and Corn Festival, Agricultural Grounds, Agassiz, (604) 796-2221

For further information on events and attractions in the area, contact the Harrison Travel Infocentre at (604) 796-3425.

Did you know?
Harrison Lake is the largest lake in southwestern British Columbia. It was used by the native people as a trade route to the Interior. This pristine 65-km-long lake was formed during the last ice age.

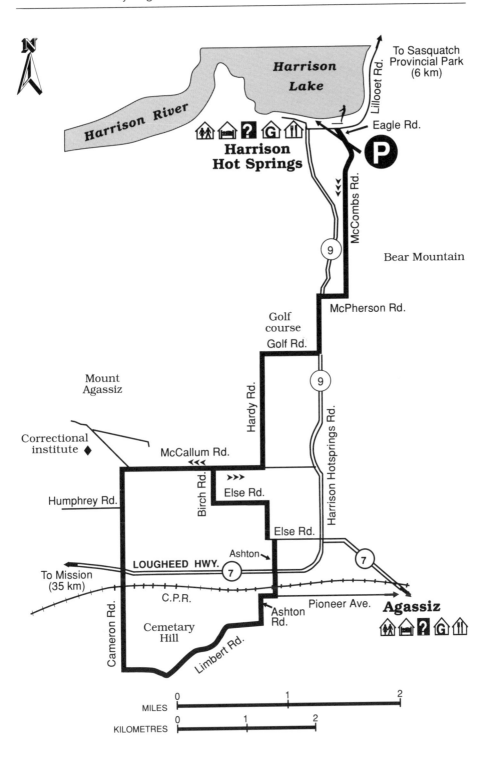

A Selection of Books Published by Gordon Soules Book Publishers

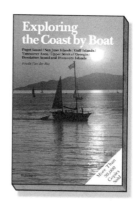

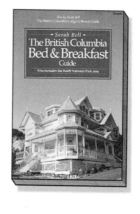

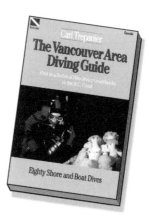

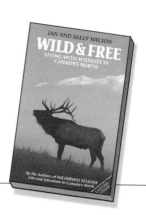